INSIDE THE WORLD'S
MOST FAMOUS
INTELLIGENCE AGENCIES

# Inside Germany's BND

## The Federal
## Intelligence Service

### Katy Schiel

The Rosen Publishing Group, Inc.
New York

Published in 2003 by The Rosen Publishing Group, Inc.
29 East 21st Street, New York, NY 10010

First Edition

**Library of Congress Cataloging-in-Publication Data**
Schiel, Katy.
Inside Germany's BND: the Federal Intelligence Service / by Katy Schiel.
    p. cm. — (Inside the world's most famous intelligence agencies)
Summary: Introduces Germany's Federal Intelligence Service, or Bundesnachrichtendienst, which once kept watch on East Germany and the Soviet bloc, but was infiltrated with counterspies in the 1950s.
Includes bibliographical references and index.
ISBN 0-8239-3813-1 (lib. bdg.)
1. Germany. Bundesnachrichtendienst—Juvenile literature. 2. Secret service—Germany—History—Juvenile literature. 3. Intelligence service—Germany—History—Juvenile literature. [1. Secret service—Germany—History. 2. Intelligence service—History. 3. Espionage—History.] I. Title. II. Series.
HV8208.7.B86 .S34 2002
327.1243—dc21

                                                    2002007364

*Manufactured in the United States of America*

**Cover image:** The new BND headquarters in Munich-Pullach, Germany, where information collected from around the world is compiled and analyzed. Based on their findings, BND agents prepare daily reports, including political evaluations, for the offices of the chancellor, the foreign and interior ministers, and other high-ranking officials.

# INSIDE THE WORLD'S MOST FAMOUS INTELLIGENCE AGENCIES

# Contents

# Introduction

The German intelligence agency BND (which stands for Bundesnachrichtendienst, or Federal Intelligence Service) watches over the wealthiest and most populous nation in Europe today. Germany is a key player in Europe's economic, political, and defense communities, and her population enjoys all of the benefits of a prosperous lifestyle—good education and medical care, a strong economy, and a progressive, artistic, and intellectual culture.

But things haven't always been so good for the people of Germany. The twentieth century was often dark and bloody. From 1914 to 1918, the country was torn apart by World War I. The 1920s were a time of desperate poverty and chaos. And in the 1930s, a ruthless dictator named Adolf Hitler came to power with his Nazi Party. Hitler's secret police, the Gestapo, terrorized the German people, taking away many of their freedoms and executing millions of Jews and everyone else deemed enemies of the state. The Nazis' determination to take over Europe set off World War II. Millions more innocent men, women, and children were killed, and many beautiful old cities, such as Dresden and Leipzig, were almost completely destroyed by bombs.

But the Germans, thanks to the support from their former enemies, such as the United States, recovered from the wars and terror. They set up a new government that has committed itself to the ideals of democracy and put safeguards in place to prevent people like Adolf Hitler from ever

In this 1918 photo, children are lined up for food from a food kitchen in post–World War I Germany.

gaining power again. Until 1989, this democracy existed only in the western part of Germany. The eastern zone was another story.

During World War II (1939–1945), Germany brutally invaded the Union of Soviet Socialist Republics (USSR). Over 20 million Soviet men, women, and children were killed in the conflict. After World War II ended in 1945, the victorious Allied armies of the United States, France, Britain, and the USSR took over Germany and divided it into four zones. The United States, France, and Britain took the western zones, while the Soviets took the eastern zone.

Despite being on the Allied side during the war, the Communist-led Soviet Union became hostile to the West. In 1949, Germany was officially split in two. The western zones

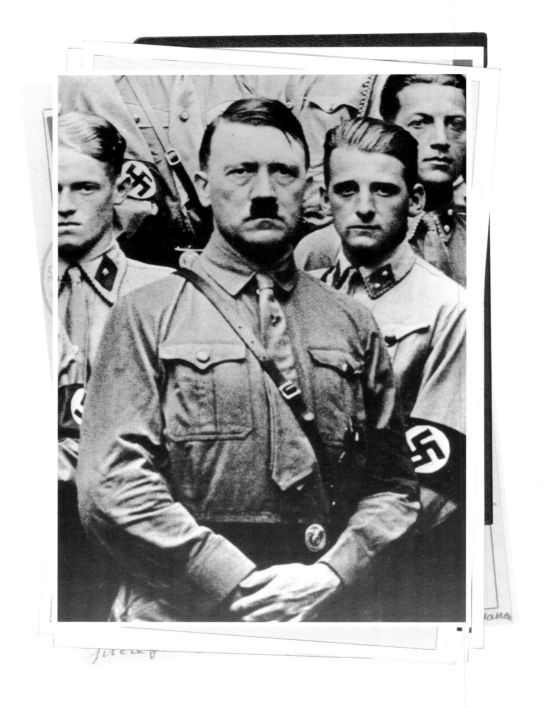

Nazi leader Adolf Hitler is shown here with soldiers in 1934. By 1935, 60 percent of all young German men, including boys as young as ten, had joined Hitler's youth movement. In it, they learned the Nazi way of thinking, especially hatred of Jews, whom Hitler blamed for Germany's poverty and religious problems.

## Timeline

1939  World War II begins

1941  The United States enters the war

1942  Reinhard Gehlen is appointed head of the FHO

May 1945  Germany surrenders

August 1945  Japan surrenders, World War II ends

1946–1947  The Cold War begins

1947  The Gehlen Organization is formed

1950  The Stasi is formed in East Germany

1956  The BND becomes the official intelligence-gathering agency of West Germany

1961  The Berlin Wall is constructed and Berlin becomes a divided city

1963  Heinz Felfe is put on trial for espionage

1967  The Six-Day War occurs in Israel

1968  Soviets invade Czechoslovakia

1968  Reinhard Gehlen retires, Gerhard Wessel becomes president of the BND

1974  Guillaume scandal breaks

1989  The Berlin Wall falls

1991  The USSR breaks up, and the Cold War ends

1997  Liechtenstein money-laundering and plutonium-smuggling scandals break in the news

September 2001  Terrorists attack the United States

The Nazis invaded Russia in June 1941. In this photo from December 1942, Russian soldiers patrol the streets in Stalingrad looking for German soldiers who may be hiding in the bombed and burned ruins.

became the Federal Republic of Germany (FRG), and the eastern zone became the misleadingly named German Democratic Republic (GDR).

The German Democratic Republic was, in fact, a rigidly controlled Communist police state. Under the USSR's influence, personal and political freedom was completely eliminated. For the next forty years, the East German people had to live under a brutal regime that made life a never-ending struggle. They were watched constantly by the secret police, the Stasi, and were rarely allowed to travel abroad or communicate with the outside world.

From 1949 until 1989, when the Communists finally lost power in East Germany, West Germany was on the

After the Berlin Wall was built in 1961 to separate East and West Berlin, more than 25,000 people managed to escape from Communist-ruled East Berlin. But not everyone was lucky. In this photo from 1962, East German police carry away the body of an eighteen-year-old killed by a hail of bullets as he tried to escape into West Berlin.

Did You Know?

Germany occupies an area slightly smaller than Montana but has 82 million more people!

front lines of the Cold War. The Cold War was not a traditional war. There were no bombs dropped or shots fired directly between the Soviets and the United States. Instead, it was a period of very high tension and alert. People on both sides were afraid that war could break out at any time, and it almost did. This is why the BND was so important not only to West Germany but also to the United States. Its role was to keep an unblinking eye on what was happening in East Germany and the whole Soviet bloc so that the Western powers would always know what was going on in those countries.

For years the BND did its job very well. It made many breakthrough discoveries of top-secret information and even influenced the young CIA (Central Intelligence Agency, the U.S. intelligence service). But then came the stumbles. In the 1950s, people found out that the BND was actually filled with spies from the East—the very people the organization was supposed to be watching! There was one disaster after another—scandals, security leaks, and accusations. The BND was in big trouble.

Through recent organizational shifts and new priorities, however, the BND has begun to re-create itself as a world-class organization. Still, the struggling agency is not always highly regarded in the world intelligence community. Whether or not the BND will regenerate itself into a top-notch agency such as the CIA or Britain's MI6 remains to be seen.

# Chapter One

# The Org Is Born

The roots of the BND go all the way back to World War II. When Adolf Hitler's forces were fighting their war of aggression in the USSR, the Nazi government needed all the information it could get about its Soviet enemies. This is when a Nazi group called the FHO (for Fremde Heere Ost, or Foreign Armies East) became active. The FHO collected all the secret information it could get about the Soviets through its large network of military and civilian informers. Data about troop movements, factory locations, military strategy, and even civilian morale was used by the FHO to gain the advantage and win battles against the Soviets.

The head of the FHO was a man named Major General Reinhard Gehlen. Toward the end of the conflict, Gehlen became disillusioned with the war and with Hitler's leadership. He realized that Hitler could not defeat the superior Allied forces.

In the autumn of 1944, Gehlen and a group of his senior officers microfilmed all of the information they had obtained about the USSR and buried it in steel boxes in the Austrian Alps. Soon after that, in May 1945, Gehlen and his men surrendered to the Americans. They were quickly arrested and put into a POW (prisoner of war) camp.

But the crafty Gehlen had a plan. He knew that the Americans would want to see the secret information he had

Reinhard Gehlen, considered one of the world's greatest spymasters, is in the center of this 1945 photo showing the staff of the Wehrmacht counter-intelligence unit.

buried in the Alps. And he was right. High-ranking American generals soon found out about the FHO and the mysterious General Gehlen, and demanded to know where he was being kept. After six weeks, the Americans found Gehlen in the POW camp and released him.

When the war was finally over, the victorious armies of the West prepared to go home. Gehlen knew from all of his intelligence work with the FHO how big a threat the USSR might be to the United States in the future. He had seen its massive military buildup and knew that the Soviets were keeping their military large to push their way into the eastern parts of Europe, including Czechoslovakia, Poland, Hungary, Romania, Bulgaria, and Germany.

If nothing were done, Gehlen told the Americans, the Soviets might invade countries like France and Britain. He had all of the evidence to prove it, buried in the Alps.

Gehlen worked out a deal: He would share what he knew with the Americans if they allowed him to continue his espionage work in the USSR and stay on as leader of western Germany's new intelligence agency. The United States realized that it did not have a good way to collect intelligence about the Soviet Union, its former wartime ally. With his bargaining chip in place, Gehlen negotiated an agreement that would allow him to lead the postwar intelligence organization despite his former involvement with the Nazis.

His group became known as the Gehlen Organization, or the Org for short. This spy network of 350 agents was led by Gehlen, but it was ultimately controlled by the United States. The Org was to be the eyes and ears of the United States in postwar Eastern Europe and the rest of the USSR for many years to come.

## Strategic Priorities

The first priority of the Org was to know where the Soviet armed forces were at all times in order to protect the 400,000 American, British, and French troops stationed in Europe. The Org also needed to learn what the Soviets were planning to do in Europe and the rest of the world, and what kinds of weapons they were developing. This was very important information, but perhaps Gehlen overestimated the Soviet military might. Some historians now think that he kept the United States on too high a state of alert, making the

## Pullach: A Great Big Secret-Service Family

Since 1947, a little town called Pullach in southern Germany has been the center of German intelligence. It was there that the Gehlen Organization (later the BND) took over a compound of about twenty buildings and set up shop. Joining the first agents were their wives, children, and pets. As this was the 1940s, most of the agents were men. Wives worked as secretaries, cooks, and schoolteachers inside the compound. Today there are many women who work in high-level positions.

Everyone ate their meals, slept, and worked within the walls of the Pullach home base. It was one big secret-service family. It has been said that Gehlen himself liked to play matchmaker with his staff, creating more "spy families" for his agency. In 2000, the BND slowly started moving operations to Germany's capital city, Berlin. They now have offices in both locations.

world situation much worse than it needed to be. Many people now say that Gehlen exaggerated how dangerous the USSR was to make himself seem more important and further his own career. But at the time, the Americans believed everything he told them. In fact, over 70 percent of America's information on the Soviet military came from Reinhard Gehlen and his Org during the years right after World War II.

The biggest priority for the Gehlen Organization was to build a comprehensive intelligence network in the USSR. The information it gathered from this group would enable West Germany to keep a knowledgeable eye on any developments in the east. The Org soon grew from 350 agents to a staff of

In June 1953, 100,000 workers rose up against Soviet rule in East Berlin. But they were quickly crushed by Soviet tanks and troops, who killed 40 people and seriously injured 125. As a top priority, the BND tracked the movements of the Soviet army at all times.

over 4,000 agents. As officers of the German army and SS (or Schutzstaffel, the elite corps of Hitler's Nazis) were released from prisoner of war camps, the Org would quickly recruit them.

## Early Successes

The first of the Org's great successes came in the Soviet zone of Germany, which would soon officially become East Germany. Gehlen's Org was able to out-spy the other Western intelligence organizations and gather more and better information because its main focus was in its own back-yard—East Germany. The Org could recruit agents more

## Tools of the Trade

The Org's branches masqueraded as business firms, often using bland company names, such as South German Sales Ltd. or Used Oil Sales. Sometimes these fake companies were in storefronts that masked the spying of secret agents. But often agents hid behind real businesses, like insurance agencies, hairdressers, tax advisory companies, or employment agencies. While customers were in the front of the store getting haircuts, agents were in the back room deciphering code or listening to Soviet radio communications. These "covers" were all over West Germany.

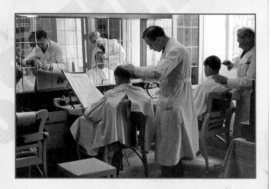

A barber shop, like this one in Hamburg, Germany, in 1955 would have been the ideal "front" for an intelligence-gathering operation.

Another popular security tool was the "dead letter box." This was a box where an agent could leave secret information for his or her organizer. After the informant dropped the secret message into the box, a secret courier would come along, take the information, and leave a reward. This was to make sure that certain informers never actually met their organizer. Other agents met their informers inside what was called a safe house, a one- or two-bedroom apartment where organizers could talk to their spies in secret. The Org, and later the BND, kept these secret apartments all over Germany.

easily and pay off fellow Germans with great rewards for information on the Soviets. At the time, most East German citizens wanted their Soviet occupiers out, so they did whatever they could to help the Org.

## The Agent-Informer Network

The backbone of the Org was a highly developed agent-informer network. One of the earliest and most successful Org agents was a man code-named Walter Zentner who walked the city where he lived to get information from contacts he knew. Knocking on their doors, he asked if they wanted to spy for the Org. In exchange for intelligence tips, he would pay them in Western money and in other valuable forms of currency: chocolate, coffee, cigarettes, and fresh milk. With chocolate in hand, the local baker would tell him exactly how many loaves of bread he delivered to the Soviet barracks the previous day. And a washerwoman would tell him how many shirts she ironed for the Soviet officers. In this crafty way, agents of the Org could find out when and by how much the Soviets were building up their military.

Gehlen wanted his agents to know only what they needed to know, and no more. This compartmentalized method was for their safety as individuals as well as for the safety of the entire Org. The less someone knew, the less damage he or she could do if caught by the enemy. Therefore, the Org was structured so that everyone at each level knew only the agent in the level immediately above his or her own. There was so much secrecy inside the Org that agents would not know much more about the group other than the identity of their organizer.

# The Org Becomes the BND

In 1949, occupied West Germany officially became the Federal Republic of Germany. Konrad Adenauer was the first chancellor (the German equivalent of a prime minister) of the FRG. Adenauer, who liked Gehlen's intelligence work, became his main supporter in the government. Many West German

Konrad Adenauer, chancellor of Germany (pictured here in 1960), was Gehlen's main supporter in the German government.

politicians felt very uneasy about Gehlen's power. They asked why a former Nazi general would be given so much power in the new democratic government. People still ask this today. But in 1956, after nine years of successful clandestine operations, the Org was made into an official branch of the German federal government with Adenauer's blessing. It remained exactly the same organization led by Gehlen, but it was given a new name: the Bundesnachrichtendienst, or BND. This was what Gehlen had always wanted—for his organization to be a recognized branch of the federal government.

# Chapter Two

# The Nuts and Bolts of the BND

The early BND under Gehlen was a complicated jumble. Since he insisted on complete secrecy within his organization, many departments and sections did not even know that the others existed. While this was good for keeping secrets, it became messy and inefficient.

Today's BND is much different. When Gehlen retired in 1968, General Gerhard Wessel became director of the BND. Reorganizing the agency completely in 1972, Wessel took the many sections of the old BND and combined them into four departments. Since then, two departments have been added to deal with new developments in the world—terrorism and new technologies. While the structure has not changed much, the BND, once only concerned with developments in the Soviet Union, now keeps an eye on the entire world.

The BND reports directly to the German chancellor's office. Consisting of six departments led by a director, the BND was set up to gather all foreign intelligence. Its sister organization, the BfV, handles internal intelligence gathering.

## Department One: Operational Intelligence

Operational Intelligence uses the traditional intelligence gathering method HUMINT, which is short for "human intelligence." The "eyes" of the BND, Department One relies on intelligence from a network of informers across the globe. The information it gathers enables the BND to watch ethnic and religious conflicts, political and economic instabilities, and social and ecological problems of every kind. Early detection of such trends from well-informed sources is of the highest importance to the BND. This is the method of intelligence gathering that most people think of when they hear the word "espionage." In fact, the BND gathers only a small amount (about 25 percent) of its information this way.

Department One selects, trains, and controls secret informants. It pays attention to a potential informant's mental agility, creativity, reliability, and ability to keep secrets. Department One also wants its people to have a sense of responsibility, technical skills, and the ability to speak foreign languages. This is to ensure the accuracy of information received and the safety of the agents.

The early BND relied almost exclusively on this kind of intelligence gathering. To find useful information, an agent might pick through trash at Russian barracks looking for scraps of paper with Cyrillic writing on them.

Because of the complexity inside this network, Department One maintains close relationships with the intelligence services of other countries to safeguard smooth operations with friendly organizations.

## The BfV: Germany's Other Intelligence-Gathering Service

While the BND is responsible for gathering intelligence in foreign countries, the BfV (Bundesamt für Verfassungsschutz, or Federal Office for the Protection of the Constitution) is responsible for collecting intelligence within Germany. The BfV could be compared to the United States's FBI. In the 1950s, there was a rivalry between Reinhard Gehlen and Otto John, the first president of the BfV. Gehlen thought the BND should be the only agency gathering intelligence for West Germany. Despite his opposition, the BfV went on to become an important part of Germany's eyes and ears on the world. In fact, it was the BfV that gathered the most intelligence inside Germany after the September 11, 2001,

During World War II, Otto John was part of a failed German plot against Hitler. In 1954, he became head of Gehlen's rival intelligence group, the BfV. John disappeared mysteriously in 1954.

terrorist attacks in New York City and near Washington, D.C.

Like the BND, the BfV is controlled directly by the chancellor's office. Its duty, according to the government's charter, is the "acquisition and evaluation of information and intelligence . . . concerning tendencies aiming at suspension, alteration, or disturbance of the constitutional order in the Federal Republic [of Germany]."

The BfV tracks many trends that threaten Germany. Among them are ideological extremism and extremism by foreigners living in Germany. The BfV is also responsible for Germany's counterintelligence, which is the collection and evaluation of information about threats to Germany's security from foreign intelligence services.

German neo-Nazis march in Hamburg, Germany, in 2000. The banner says "Free-National . . . Resistance Lives!" Although this group was given permission to march by Germany's highest court, they, and other exremist groups, are monitored by the BfV.

## Department Two: Technical Procurement

Department Two is the "ears" of the BND. It uses a method called technical procurement to filter intelligence from the international communication stream of foreign countries. Called "open sources," this technique of surveillance is termed SIGINT, from "signal intelligence." The SIGINT method is more expensive than

## The School of the BND

Do you want to work for the BND? The agency has its own school, located in Department Four. Highly specialized intelligence requires specialized knowledge and talents. The job of the school is to provide BND agents with both general and specific training to prepare them for the situations that they will face on the job. For example, an agent being placed in Russia will be given intensive classes in the Russian language. Or an agent sent to investigate underwater espionage will be given scuba diving lessons. The school of the BND, which accepts students from many fields, teaches journalism, combat, encryption, computer programming, foreign languages, and much more.

HUMINT, but it is more efficient. With machines that never get tired, Department Two can monitor electronic information around the clock. In this way, SIGINT can supplement or even replace human agents. Like all modern intelligence agencies, the BND gains about 75 percent of its information from open electronic sources. As electronic communication becomes more widespread, the BND faces more challenges. Out of 100,000 electronic reports that might come into their offices, only about 450 would be considered useful!

## Department Three: Evaluation

Department Three is the "brain" of the agency. Encompassing the BND's entire intelligence work chain, Department Three is the beginning and end of everything

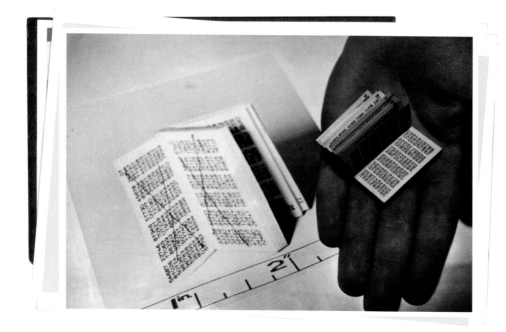

This miniature code book from 1968 contains groups of numbers that spies used to decipher messages from Moscow.

happening within the agency. The federal government orders information that it wants through this department. The staff of Department Three passes the work orders to Department One and Department Two.

When the information has been gathered, it is carefully examined by the staff of Department Three. Secret messages intercepted by agents and machines, along with any other information that has been picked up, are analyzed. Agents with Department Three review the information carefully to predict future trends and events and to get a picture of the world situation as a whole. This data is passed along to officials of the federal government who dispense it to the officials who need it.

This still photo, dated June 19, 2002, is said to be from a video created by Osama bin Laden at a military training camp at al-Faruq in Afghanistan.

## Department Four: Administration, Law, and Central Services

The administrative and educational branch, Department Four, is the "heart" of the BND. The staff of Department Four does all of the personnel management: hiring, paying, feeding, counseling, and planning for the other departments. Department Four oversees the planning and administration for the BND.

## Department Five: Organized Crime and International Terrorism

Department Five is concerned with problems of organized crime and international terrorism. For the BND, these threats are the most dangerous because the perpetrators do not behave like conventional enemies. Organized crime groups and international terrorists do not have regular armies with clear front lines. Instead, they have many layers. Groups such as Al Qaeda have shown how complicated it can be to trace a terrorist organization.

Department Five analyzes and acts upon any threats to Germany or any other country. Because of the complexity of these problems, Department Five members are meant to work closely with the security agencies of other countries.

International cooperation can ensure that all information is shared correctly.

## Department Six: Technical Support

Intelligence agencies always need the newest and best technology. This is where the staff of Department Six comes in. Department Six handles everything from practical computer support to high-level technical innovation. This is the staff that makes sure that everything technical is running smoothly in the BND. The main function of Department Six is to supply and operate communications systems that can provide fast, safe, worldwide transfer of information. They also run what is called an "IT architecture," which links every imaginable technical piece of the agency.

Some of the areas that Department Six deals with are data processing, telecommunications, chemistry, and physics. This department contains workshops and laboratories that produce and analyze new technologies, since technology needs to be upgraded constantly.

# Chapter Three

# The BND: The 1940s Through the 1960s

Some historians say the BND was at its best in its early days. Through the late 1940s and mid-1950s, when it was still called the Gehlen Organization, the young intelligence agency was on a roller-coaster ride that only seemed to go up. Fueled by the early urgency of the new Cold War tensions, the BND was out-spying every other Western intelligence agency around. It secured one major victory after another.

Conditions were especially bad in East Germany, and most people were desperately poor. It was very easy for the Org to recruit agents during this time. Also, the East German government had not yet built up its tight spy web, so it was easier to obtain secret information.

One of the first major successes for the Org came in 1948, when it learned from an agent named Klaus Imhoff that East Germany was remilitarizing, or building up its military again after World War II. Since this came as a complete surprise to the West, it was a big victory for the young agency.

In 1948, the Org recruited a key East German politician named Hermann Moritz Wilhelm Kastner. As vice president of East Germany, Kastner was a very influential man. Once he had been lured over to the western side, he began to tell secret after secret. This was a great coup and a major source of information for the Org.

In 1949, the Russians created the ground-breaking MiG-15, pictured above. In 1953, the U.S. Far East Command offered a $100,000 reward to the person who delivered this plane to them. For months, no one took up their offer until a twenty-one-year-old senior lieutenant in the North Korean Air Force landed a MiG-15 in South Korea. Unaware of the award, he had decided to defect to South Korea because, according to the U.S. Air Force Web site, he "was sick and tired of the red deceit."

Yet another success came in 1949, when Org agents discovered that the Soviet Union had invented a new kind of spy plane, the MiG-15. One able agent of the Gehlen Organization was able to determine what kind of fuel the Soviets used to power the MiG-15. Sneaking onto a train that was carrying MiG-15 fuel, the agent lowered a beer bottle into the tank. When he pulled up the bottle, he had a sample of the secret jet fuel in hand.

By 1956, when the Org became the BND and was made an official part of the West German government, its luck began to run out. From the mid-1950s on, Gehlen and his secret service made a series of impressive blunders. People began to doubt their efficiency as well as their usefulness.

Many experts say that Gehlen was to blame. After all, he had been a Nazi, and his dictatorial methods of running the BND were grossly out of step with changing times. It was revealed that while the BND had many spies planted in East Germany, the East Germans had just as many spies planted in the West German government!

In East Germany, the secret intelligence organization was the Ministry for State Security, or Stasi. A ruthless organization that abused its power and spied on its own people, the Stasi had spies everywhere—even listening in on confessions in churches! This treachery was a huge blow to West Germany in general and to the BND in particular.

## The Felfe Affair

Probably the most harmful mole, or counterspy, inside the BND was Heinz Felfe. Like Gehlen, Felfe began his career as a Nazi intelligence officer. At the end of the war, Felfe gained access to the Org through the "old-boy network" of ex-officers. But Felfe was actually working for the Soviets. Once inside of the Org, Felfe quickly climbed up the ranks into influential positions. One of the most important jobs he performed for his Soviet bosses was to spread "disinformation," or false information, around the BND. Felfe used his secret knowledge of Soviet intelligence to improve his own position within the BND. He liked to brag about knowing exactly where and when one high-ranking Soviet officer would use the bathroom!

Felfe became Gehlen's favorite agent, and he trusted him with everything. But secretly, Felfe took everything he learned from Gehlen and passed it directly to Moscow. In this way, he blew many BND agents' covers, leading to their arrests or sometimes even to their deaths.

For such a smart spy, Felfe was caught doing something very foolish. He purchased a very expensive house that he could never have afforded on his BND salary. Other BND agents, who did not like him and suspected him of being a double agent, exposed him. His treachery cost the BND many years of work. The

Reinhard Gehlen, who had spied on the Russians for Hitler, cleverly traded what he had learned as a Nazi to the Americans in exchange for immunity from punishment.

damage to the BND's carefully established networks and channels inside the Soviet sphere was enormous. And the finger of blame was pointed right at Gehlen.

The Felfe Affair was the beginning of the end for Gehlen's reputation and career. His life's work was in ruins. Many said that it was Gehlen's fault not only that Felfe was hired but also that he rose through the ranks so quickly. Gehlen had relied on an old-boy network for the hiring and not on common-sense security clearance. His outmoded, closed-minded ways of leadership had caused irreparable damage to the BND.

Gehlen was allowed to finish his remaining years of service for the BND. The "Grand Old Man" retired in 1968, worn-out and tired at the age of sixty-six. What began as a spectacular career in the postwar years ended in disgrace.

## The Stasi

After the Soviets took over, East Germany resembled a huge prison where only the prison wardens lived well. The wardens were officers of the East German secret police, or Stasi. While the East German people shivered and starved, members of the Stasi lived like kings as they kept an iron grip on the terrorized population. Their methods for squashing dissent were so ruthless and efficient that even the notorious KGB, the infamous Soviet intelligence organization, was disgusted by the Stasi's methods.

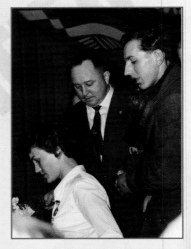

Erich Mielke *(left)* stands behind Helga Haase, East Germany's first female Olympic speed skating champion at a reception for East German ice stars in 1960.

From 1950, when it was founded, until its long-awaited death in 1990, the Stasi wove a giant web of spies and agents around the world. It has been estimated that there was one Stasi spy for every seven people in East Germany! Not only did the Stasi have a huge network inside of East Germany, but it also managed to enlist over 30,000 West Germans, including a number of BND agents. In fact, the Stasi was a major obstacle to the BND throughout the Cold War, repeatedly thwarting its carefully conceived plans.

The Stasi was led for its forty years by Erich Mielke, who began his career by murdering two policemen in a political stunt as a teenager. After World War II ended and the Communists seized power, Mielke quickly became head of the new secret police organization. Mielke's methods for his Stasi included the obsessive surveillance of the entire population. The Stasi used its special "mailmen"—spies stationed at every post office in East Germany—to open every piece of mail coming from the West. Suspicious letters were chemically treated to uncover the possibility of messages written in invisible ink. Other envelopes were examined under microscopes to search for hidden messages.

Another Stasi tactic was to use brutal physical and psychological torture on anyone suspected of being a dissident. One unlucky victim of the Stasi was a young student named Horst Erdmann. After distributing leaflets to his classmates calling for free elections, Erdmann was arrested and spent eight years under terrible conditions in prison.

Despite its round-the-clock watch on the residents of East Germany, however, Stasi agents were not able to predict the uprising in 1989 that finally brought down the Berlin Wall and the hated Stasi regime.

## The Berlin Wall Blunder

Besides being riddled with spies, the BND was making other major mistakes. On August 13, 1961, one of the defining moments in German—if not world—history occurred with the building of the Berlin Wall. And the BND did not even predict it. In fact, only two days before, on August 11, the BND had issued a report to Berlin mayor Willy Brandt that the East Germans were not planning to do anything that weekend. They were completely wrong, and West German politicians began calling for the end of the BND.

A construction worker helps build the Berlin Wall in 1961. It was a major blunder for West Germany's BND to have missed all signs that East Germany was about to erect a wall to separate the people and the governments of the politically divided city.

The BND successfully predicted the Six-Day War in 1967 in which Israel took control of Bethlehem. Here, an Israeli soldier marches a Jordanian captive through the streets because he did not have identification papers.

## A Success! Predicting the Six-Day War

But politicians had to admit the BND was doing some things right. While it was not at its best in predicting political events in Germany like the construction of the Berlin Wall, the BND correctly predicted some military activity. In June 1967, the BND predicted that Israel would attack Egypt, Syria, and Jordan. This attack began a war in the Middle East that lasted exactly 132 hours and 30 minutes, almost six days. So it was named the Six-Day War. Not only did the BND correctly predict that Israel would attack, but it even knew the hour that it would happen!

Using radio-reconnaissance to spy on the Soviet army, the BND predicted the Russian invasion of Czechoslovakia. In this 1968 photo, young Czechs carry their flag as a show of national pride while Soviet tanks burn.

## Another Success! Predicting the Invasion of Czechoslovakia

Another success for the BND came in 1968, when its agents correctly predicted that the USSR would invade Czechoslovakia. Even though they were under Soviet domination, the Czech people were enjoying a short period of relative freedom, complete with free speech and the return of democracy. This was known as the Prague Spring. The Soviets watched this with anger, and finally, in August 1968, they had enough. The BND listened to Soviet troop movements for days and correctly predicted that Soviet troops would attack Prague, the capital city. The Prague Spring had come to an end, and the BND saw it coming.

# The End of an Era

Despite its successes, the BND was largely in disgrace by the end of the 1960s. Now that Gehlen was gone, a new leadership was stepping up to the plate. Would they be able to correct the mistakes of the past and bring the BND up to the level of its sister agencies throughout Western Europe?

# Chapter Four

# The BND: The 1970s through 2001

When Gerhard Wessel took over the BND in 1968, the agency was in crisis. Wessel immediately made big reforms that brought together the intricate web of departments that had been run by Gehlen. He also worked hard to bring the BND's technology department up to date.

In the early days of the BND, the agent-informer network was the core of the organization. As time went on, the BND modernized its listening apparatus and added monitoring stations all over Europe. These mighty radio-reconnaissance stations were what helped the BND predict the Soviet invasion of Czechoslovakia in 1968. The BND was moving into the technological age.

Starting in 1970, technology became the BND's main priority. Camouflaged by secret code names such as SUSANNE or LERCHE, listening stations aimed at the Soviet bloc were constructed all over Germany. The BND relied more on electronic surveillance not only because it was more effective but also because it was safer for its agents.

Wessel also took major steps to intensify cooperation between the BND, German armed forces, and other Western intelligence services. Beginning in the mid-1970s, the BND, along with American, British, German, and Danish naval vessels, set up a comprehensive listening network in the Baltic Sea. As the Cold War was still dividing the West from the East, it was important for friendly nations to cooperate with each other.

## Spies, Spies, and More Spies

German chancellor Willy Brandt (born Herbert Ernst Frahm) and Gunter Guillaume prepare for the election campaign in 1974.

Although the BND seemed to be making great strides forward, the agency was still riddled with moles. One of the worst and most harmful of these Stasi counterspies was Gunter Guillaume, who was chief adviser to the prime minister. He wreaked so much havoc on the West German government that, in 1974, he brought down the Social Democratic government of Chancellor Willy Brandt, the one-time mayor of Berlin.

During this time, the BND had some successes in the spy department. From the mid-1970s until 1985, the BND received undercover information from a prominent Soviet journalist named Ilya M. Suslov, an editor for the Soviet news agency Novosti who had his own television show about space exploration. Suslov received secret information from important Soviet figures in exchange for publicity on his TV show.

Another success for the BND came in 1979. Warner Schiller was a Stasi officer who gave the BND very useful details about the structure and methods of the Stasi. His intelligence led to the arrest of Soviet bloc agents in West Germany and other Western countries.

# For Love or Money?
# The Romeo Ploy

While most spies were lured by money, some were taken in by love. One especially cruel tactic that the Stasi used to recruit moles was the "Romeo Ploy." Beginning in the 1960s, the Stasi began to enlist handsome single men throughout East Germany. These "Romeos," trained in the arts of espionage and seduction, were sent out to recruit lonely young Western women. The dashing spies would wine and dine their prey until the women fell in love with them. Then the Romeo would lie and say he was in trouble and he needed his victim to do some spying for him, "just this once." Once these young women began to spy, many of them never stopped.

One such unlucky woman was Gabriele Gast, a student from West Germany. She traveled to East Germany from time to time to conduct research on women's lives there. On one visit she was seduced by a man code-named "Karliszek." By playing on her emotions, Karliszek persuaded her to spy for the Stasi. After graduating in 1972, she got a job offer from the BND. She did well in the BND, eventually obtaining a high rank equivalent to lieutenant colonel and working directly under Chancellor Helmut Kohl. Through her, the head of the

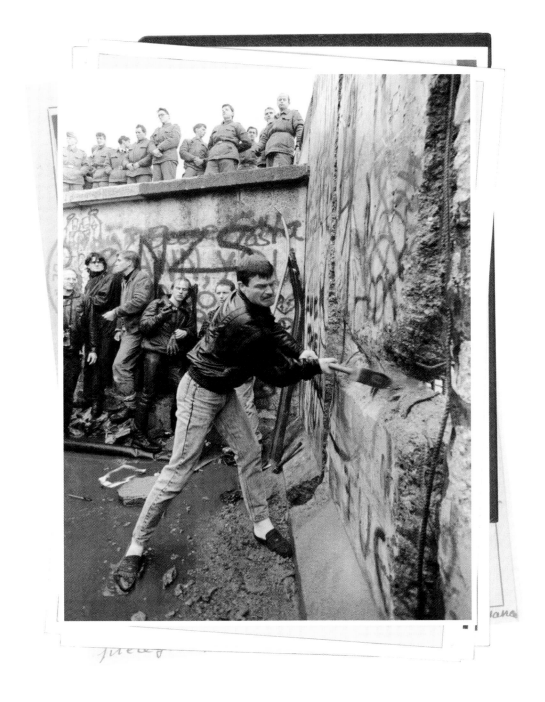

At the end of September 1989, East Berliners began mass demonstrations against the Soviet government and system. On November 9, 1989, the Berlin Wall was opened by the newly installed East German government. In this picture from November 11, 1989, a demonstrator takes a hammer to the Berlin Wall as East Berlin border guards watch from above.

Stasi was able to read the chancellor's daily intelligence mail every day! A tip-off to the BND in 1994 led to her arrest. Treated well by the courts, she was sentenced to only six years in prison.

## The Plutonium Affair

It was supposed to be a huge intelligence success for the BND. In 1994, BND agents caught three men smuggling weapons-grade plutonium from Russia into Germany at the Munich airport. But soon the real story came out. The BND had set up the whole plot to create good publicity for itself. Undercover BND agents had paid the men to smuggle dangerous plutonium on a commercial airline, endangering the lives of everyone on board. This was a terrible abuse of human rights. When the story came out, there was a huge uproar, and the BND was once again caught in a scandal.

## The End of the Cold War

The Berlin Wall was toppled in 1989, and two years later, in 1991, the USSR fell apart. The Cold War was finally over! The Stasi, arch enemy to the BND, was destroyed. BND staff wondered what would come next.

In the years after the Cold War, Germany, like all Western nations, faced changed priorities. After all, there was no more Soviet bloc to spy on. In 1994, the federal government assigned the BND two new missions: to watch over money laundering and the international drug trade.

The towers of New York City's World Trade Center burn on September 11, 2001, after being hit by two hijacked airplanes. American intelligence agencies and intelligence agencies around the world were baffled by the terrorists' ability to pull off this horrific attack without detection.

## Gunter Guillaume: Master Stasi Spy

In 1955, Gunter Guillaume was a Stasi agent who wormed his way into the West German political scene. Through cunning and hard work, he ruthlessly rose through higher and higher political ranks, easily passing the BND's security checks. His wife, Christel, also a Stasi spy, worked as a secretary for a very influential local politician and was in a great position to steal many secrets. They spent their evenings photographing sensitive documents with spy cameras. They reported to their Stasi bosses on secret radio waves.

In 1969, Guillaume got a very important job in the chancellery of West Germany. He was regarded as completely trustworthy and hardworking. As a result, the Stasi had an agent in one of the most important government organizations in the world. A few years later, he climbed the ladder again when he was appointed as one of three assistants to Willy Brandt, who was then chancellor of West Germany. This would be the equivalent of a foreign spy becoming deputy assistant to the president of the United States!

Guillaume traveled everywhere with his new boss, at every turn leaking critical information to the East. He supplied the Stasi with situation reports from the BND and supplied them with minutes from meetings between Brandt and world leaders. The damage this one man did to West Germany was impossible to measure.

In 1974, after being watched carefully by the BND, Guillaume was finally caught. He and his wife were so good at their jobs that until they were arrested, their eighteen-year-old son, Pierre, did not know that his parents were spies! In 1981, the Guillaumes were released in exchange for eight West German spies who were caught in East Germany. Returning to the East, they were welcomed as heroes.

# The BND Uncovers a Money-Laundering Ring

In 1997, the BND succeeded in a major intelligence coup when it discovered that a major money laundering operation existed in the principality of Liechtenstein. Money laundering is hiding, moving, and investing the proceeds of criminal conduct to make that money appear "clean." A tiny country that takes up only 62 square miles and has 32,000 people, wealthy Liechtenstein was home to bankers who were involved in seriously illegal dealings.

Every night the BND listened to the banks' data exchange. From this, they figured out that groups from Mafia organizations to drug cartels were hiding their money in Liechtenstein's banks. And the bankers knew they were doing it, which is what made the whole scandal so frightening. Were they also hiding terrorist funds? Perhaps, but the story is still being sorted out by the BND.

# Warnings About Terrorism

In September 2001, the unthinkable happened in the United States. Terrorists hijacked commercial aircraft and crashed them into the World Trade Center towers in New York City and the Pentagon outside of Washington, D.C., killing thousands of people and catching the United States completely off guard. A fourth hijacked plane, apparently headed for another American landmark, crashed in Pennsylvania, killing everyone aboard.

German chancellor Helmut Kohl, shown here in 1985, was a victim of Stasi spying, as BND double agent Gabriele Gast turned over Kohl's daily intelligence mail to East Germany.

Then it was revealed that the alleged terrorists had used Hamburg, Germany, as the staging ground for the attacks. The German intelligence agencies, including the BND and the BfV, had not been able to determine exactly what was going on right under their noses. However, German intelligence had learned that something terrible was going to take place in America. In June 2001, three months before the attacks, the BND warned the CIA and Israel that terrorists from the Middle East were planning to hijack commercial aircraft to use as weapons to attack "important symbols of American and Israeli culture." The BND was right on the mark.

# Chapter Five

# Today's BND

Like all modern nations, Germany needs an early-warning system to protect itself from dangerous developments from abroad. This is where the BND can be crucial. As the BND enters the new millennium, it must fight to remain effective and relevant.

The fall of the Soviet Union and the end of the Cold War in the early 1990s did not make the BND's job easier. Instead, new enemies and challenges have emerged to take the place of the USSR. These dangerous groups and countries are less predictable than the USSR was. With this in mind, the need for better intelligence is even more crucial. The attacks of September 11, 2001, make this very clear.

The BND must constantly reshape its priorities and focus as world politics change. The BND of today does not want to make the same mistakes as the old, inefficient BND under Reinhard Gehlen. The urgent, new priorities that have surfaced since the end of the Cold War represent new challenges for Germany, as well as for the entire community of democratic states.

In addition, Germany is now considering a reevaluation of its own privacy laws, which were put in place to prevent the kinds of abuses that the German people suffered under the undemocratic regimes in the past.

The BND's priorities at the beginning of the twenty-first century include working to end:

- The illegal use of technology
- International terrorism
- International organized crime
- International arms traffic
- Illegal immigration

The BND has been carefully watching the misuse of technology as it relates to national security. According to the BND, computer viruses are becoming standard weapons in international conflicts. As computers become more important to the world's economies and militaries, they must be more carefully monitored for illegal activity. The BND has been closely watching new technologies and how they can be manipulated by armies of "hacker soldiers."

# International Terrorism

In April 2001, the BND issued a warning that Iraq was producing a new class of chemical weapons. The information was based on intelligence from several German companies that had delivered components for these weapons to Baghdad. Long before the September 11 terrorist attacks, the BND was carefully monitoring terrorist Osama bin Laden. Combined with the prediction that terrorists from the Middle East were planning to stage attacks using commercial airplanes, the BND is proving to be chillingly correct in its intelligence work.

Chancellor Helmut Kohl *(right)* and Interior Minister Manfred Kanther of Germany are shown here in January 1998 as the Bonn Parliament debates the highly controversial bill that would give German police the freedom to use electronic surveillance in private homes. When the bill passed by four votes, an opposing member of Parliament called it "Black Friday" for Germany's constitution.

Since the 1940s, privacy laws in Germany have been very strict, making it more difficult for German intelligence to spy on its own people. After the September 11 terrorist attacks, the BND and its sister intelligence organization, the BfV, gained more power to collect intelligence. These powers include listening in on suspected terrorists' telephone calls without going through a lot of paperwork. How much more power and freedom to snoop the German government grants its intelligence organizations remains to be seen.

**Did You Know?**

Les Aspin, the chair of the House Armed Services Committee under President Bill Clinton, first used the term "rogue states" in the 1990s to describe Cuba, North Korea, Iran, Iraq, and Libya. These nations oppose the United States's foreign and military policies in their regions. The term "rogue states" has now become part of government and media jargon.

## International Organized Crime

The BND's discovery of money laundering in Liechtenstein was a major success for the agency. By keeping a keen eye on organized crime, especially when it is linked to terrorism, the BND may be able to earn a solid reputation as a world-class agency.

## International Arms Traffic

During the Cold War, only a few countries possessed weapons of mass destruction. Now many countries have made or are capable of possessing these weapons. The BND is carefully watching who is building which weapons. Although the United States is by far the largest seller of weapons, the BND has focused primarily on the rogue states: Iraq, Libya, and North Korea.

North Korea has been a key supplier of weapons and components to other rogue nations. Even though the North Korean people are starving, the government still makes a lot

After the September 11, 2001, terrorist attacks, this wanted poster was created in English and Arabic. The photos depict two men associated with leading hijacking suspect Mohammed Atta. Since the two men had lived in Hamburg, Germany, the German crime agency said it would hang more than 25,000 posters throughout the country.

of money selling weapons to countries with large cash reserves. According to the BND, Libya is acquiring weapons components that would allow it to attack targets as far away as Germany.

# Illegal Immigration

As the borders of Europe open to one another in a new era of unity, what the BND calls the "growing threat" of illegal immigration has worsened. A top priority for the BND is to curb the tide of people who enter the country illegally. Many of these people come from countries such as Turkey, Iraq, and China, where money and opportunities are not as plentiful as they are in Germany. According to the BND,

One night in 1999, this Romanian man tried to enter Germany illegally from the Czech Republic. Police handcuffed him to a wall until they could question him.

many of these illegal immigrants are smuggled in to Germany with the help of organized crime organizations, which charge desperately poor people from $5,000 to $15,000 to be transported under terrible conditions that sometimes result in their deaths. The BND is currently fighting for a higher budget to hire Turkish- and Arabic-speaking people who could penetrate the groups that run these illicit businesses.

## The BND Looks Toward the Future

From a top-notch intelligence agency to an international laughing stock, the BND has been through it all. But the world's constantly shifting political climate and a new spirit of international cooperation offers many chances for the BND to regain its fine reputation in the coming years. Will it take advantage of these opportunities and rejoin the highly regarded community of Western intelligence agencies? Only time will tell.

# Glossary

**agent**  A representative or official of a government or administrative department of a government.

**Berlin Wall**  The wall built by the Communist East German government in 1961 to separate East Berlin from free West Berlin. The wall was torn down in 1989.

**clandestine**  Secret.

**Cold War**  The undeclared war between the Soviet Union and the United States in which each country sought to promote the spread of its government's ideas.

**Communism**  A system of government where the state controls the means of production, and a single, authoritarian party holds power.

**counterintelligence**  Keeping important information from an enemy, often by providing wrong information.

**cover**  An agent in disguise.

**Cyrillic**  The alphabet used in Russian, Bulgarian, and certain other Slavic languages.

**dead letter box**  A secret location where an informer leaves information for an agent, and vice versa.

**dictator**  Someone who is an absolute ruler.

**disinformation**  False information created to mislead an enemy.

**drug cartel**  A combination of independent organizations formed so that its members can regulate production, pricing, and marketing of illegal drugs.

**East Berlin**  The Communist-controlled eastern portion of Berlin that was physically separated from West Berlin from 1961 to 1989 by the Berlin Wall.

**encryption**  A message that has been put into code or cipher.

**espionage**  The act of using spies to obtain secret information about a country, group, or company.

**Gestapo**  The German internal security police as organized under the Nazi regime, known for its terrorist methods directed against those suspected of treason or questionable heritage or loyalty.

**Hitler, Adolf**  The Nazi dictator who ruled Germany from 1933 until 1945.

**informer**  A person who reveals secret information, especially one who reveals information about others, often for compensation.

**intelligence**  Secretly gained information about an enemy.

**invisible ink**  Ink that is colorless and invisible until treated by a chemical, heat, or special light.

**microfilm**  A film on which printed materials are photographed at greatly reduced size for ease of storage.

**mole**  A spy inside an organization.

**money laundering**  To make stolen money appear legitimate.

**Nazi**  A person who practices the Nazi ideals, especially the policy of state control of the economy, racist nationalism, and national expansion.

**old-boy network**  An informal system of mutual assistance and friendship where people, mostly men belonging to a particular group, such as the alumni of a school, exchange favors and connections in business and politics.

**ploy** An action calculated to frustrate an opponent or gain an advantage indirectly or deviously; a maneuver.

**principality** A territory ruled by a prince or princess.

**secret police** A police force operating largely in secret and often using terror tactics to suppress dissent and political opposition.

**Stasi** The East German intelligence organization; also called the East German Secret Police.

**surveillance** A close watch kept on something or someone.

**tactic** A method to achieve a goal.

**telecommunication** The science and technology of communication over a distance by transmitting impulses electronically, as by telegraph, cable, telephone, radio, or television.

**terrorism** Regular use of violence, terror, and intimidation to achieve a goal.

**tip-off** A piece of confidential, advance, or inside information.

**West Berlin** The democratically controlled, western portion of Berlin that was physically separated from East Berlin by the Berlin Wall.

**worm** To penetrate an organization.

# For More Information

Goethe-Institut Boston (Information about German language
    and culture)
170 Beacon Street
Boston, MA 02116
(617) 262-6050
Web site: http://www.goethe.de/uk/bos/enindex.htm

International Spy Museum
800 F Street NW
Washington, DC 20004
(866) SPY MUSEUM (779-6873)
Web site: http://www.spymuseum.org

National Cryptologic Museum
Rt. 32 and the Baltimore-Washington Parkway
Fort Meade, MD
(301) 688-5849
Web site: http://www.nsa.gov/museum

## Web Sites

Due to the changing nature of Internet links, the Rosen
Publishing Group, Inc., has developed an online list of Web
sites related to the subject of this book. This site is
updated regularly. Please use this link to access the list:

http://www.rosenlinks.com/iwmfia/bnd/

# For Further Reading

Ali, Tariq, and Susan Watkins. *1968: Marching in the Streets*. New York: Free Press, 1998.

Epler, Doris M. *The Berlin Wall: How It Rose and Why It Fell*. Madison, WI: Demco Media, 1992.

Landau, Elaine. *Big Brother Is Watching: Secret Police and Intelligence Services*. New York: Walker & Co., 1992.

Manley, Claudia B. *Secret Agents: Life as a Professional Spy*. New York: The Rosen Publishing Group, Inc., 2001.

McKenna, David L. *East Germany*. Broomal, PA: Chelsea House, 1988.

Melton, H. Keith. *The Ultimate Spy Book*. London: Dorling Kindersley Ltd., 1996.

Moss, Francis. *The Rosenberg Espionage Case*. San Diego, CA: Lucent Books, 2000.

Resnick, Abraham. *The Union of Soviet Socialist Republics: A Survey from 1917–1991*. Chicago: Children's Press, 1992.

Spencer, William. *Germany: Then and Now*. New York: Franklin Watts, 1994.

Stewart, Gail B. *America Under Attack: September 11, 2001*. San Diego, CA: Lucent Books, 2002.

Symynkywitz, Jeffrey B. *Germany: United Again*. New York: Dillon Press, 1995.

Tunnell, Michael O. *Brothers in Valor: A Story of Resistance.* New York: Holiday House, 2001.

Wiese, Jim. *Spy Science: 40 Secret-Sleuthing, Code Cracking, Spy-Catching Activities for Kids.* New York: John Wiley & Sons, Inc., 1996.

Ziff, John. *Espionage and Treason.* Philadelphia: Chelsea House Publishers, 2000.

# Bibliography

BND's official Web site (in German, but translatable through Google). Retrieved March 2002 (http://www.bundesnachrichtendienst.de/start.htm).

CIA World Factbook. "Germany." Retrieved February 2002 (http://www.cia.gov/cia/publications/factbook/geos/gm.html).

"European Officials Warn U.S. Not to Attack Iraq." Retrieved July 2002 (http://www.vcn.bc.ca/~dastow/reu20216.txt).

BBCi. "Ex-Stasi Chief Dies." March 2000. Retrieved July 2002 (http://news.bbc.co.uk/1/hi/world/europe/764397.stm).

Federation of American Scientists. "German Intelligence." Retrieved February 2002 (http://fas.org/irp/world/germany).

Hibbs, Mark. "Fairy Tales in Munich." *Bulletin of the Atomic Scientists*, Vol. 51, November 21, 1995, p. 5.

Hohne, Heinz, and Hermann Zolling. *The General Was a Spy: The Truth About General Gehlen and His Spy Ring.* New York: Coward, McCann, 1972.

Koeler, John O. *Stasi: The Untold Story of the East German Secret Police.* Boulder, CO: Westview Press, 1999.

Krock, Lexi. "Twentieth Century Deceptions." PBS.org. Retrieved July 2002 (http://www.pbs.org/wgbh/nova/venona/deceptions.html).

Richelson, Jeffrey T. *Foreign Intelligence Organizations.* Cambridge, MA: Ballinger Publishing Co., 1988.

# Index

# Credits

## About the Author

Katy Schiel is a freelance writer who has traveled extensively through Germany and Eastern Europe. She lives with her husband in Cambridge, Massachusetts.

## Photo Credits

Cover © Mächler/DPA; pp. 5, 6, 9, 17, 25, 39 © Hulton/Archive/Getty Images, Inc.; pp. 8, 13, 16, 19, 34, 35, 36 © Bettmann/Corbis; pp. 22, 32 © Getty Images, Inc.; pp. 23, 41, 43 © Reuters NewMedia, Inc.; p. 26 © FP/Corbis; p. 29 © TimePix; pp. 31, 49, 52 © AP/Wide World Photos; p. 46 © Jacques M. Chenet/Corbis; p. 51 © Reuters/Ralph Orlowski/TimePix.

## Layout and Design

Thomas Forget

## Editor

Jill Jarnow